P9-DWY-202

DATE DUE

MY 9 '95			
JY 9 '97			
AP 7 '99			

DEMCO 38-296

Tino Villanueva

SHAKING OFF
THE DARK

ARTE PUBLICO PRESS
Houston
1984

1

ble through a grant from The
Arts, and the Texas Commis-

the following publications in
his book originally appeared:
*The American Literary Review, Caliban, Hispamérica,
Homenaje a Jorge Guillén, La Semana de Bellas Artes, Latin
American Literary Review, Literatura Chilena en Exilio,
The Ontario Review, Revista Chicano-Riqueña, Tejidos,
The Texas Quarterly, Urthona, Wellesley Wragtime, Tramp
Printers*.

Cover design by Narciso Peña.

Arte Público Press
Revista Chicano-Riqueña
University of Houston
Houston, Texas 77004

2

To my professors
in return for some seeds they
perhaps didn't know they sowed.

One day the Nouns were clustered in the street.
An Adjective walked by, with her dark beauty.
The Nouns were struck, moved, changed.
The next day a Verb drove up, and created the Sentence.

"Permanently," Kenneth Koch.

Te respondo
que todavía no sabemos
hasta cuándo o hasta dónde
puede llegar una palabra,
quién la recogerá ni de qué boca
con suficiente fe
para darle su forma verdadera.

Haber llevado el fuego un sólo instante
razón nos da la esperanza.

"No inútilmente," José Angel Valente.

CONTENTS

From Silence

History I Must Wake To

INTRODUCTION

Dios te libre, lector, de prólogos largos y malos epítetos
—Francisco de Quevedo

Shaking Off The Dark reaffirms Tino Villanueva's position among those forerunners of Chicano poets who emerged in the 60's and early 70's, a period known as the Chicano Renaissance. Appearing slightly more than a decade after his first book, *Hay Otra Voz Poems* (1972), *Shaking Off The Dark* develops and intensifies a central theme: the salvation of the individual and the social self from silence, chaos and annihilation.

The expression of these two entities of human experience-the individual and the social being—is a response to two imperatives, esthetic and moral. Villanueva affirms that the former corresponds to the "tradition of esthetic appreciation"; it is an artistic impulse that culminates in an esthetic event which gives form and expression to the revelations of the "contemplative attitude." The moral imperative is the poet's response as a human being responsible for himself and his fellow human beings. This "moral gesture" the poet calls the "conflictive attitude: the poetry of humanist affirmation."

One essential vision, however, emanates from both of these attitudes. As Bruce-Novoa affirms, "Certain oppressive forces in life threaten to relegate people to a silent, invisible and anonymous state of nonexistence." These forces can be conceived in absolute terms: Time sweeps one's "dust-bound youth" (*HOVP*) to inevitable Death and eternal Silence. The poet's response to these forces consists in the affirmation of identity and existence by three means related in their end: the voice of the individual through the written word, love and the collective voice or word of the Chicano experience.

Creativity is a vital endeavor; the poem allows access to a "resting place / on your private journey." Love, be it the erotic act with a poem or a woman, is similarly a creative act by which the partners can name and share "the strength of all things flowing." The proclamation of the collective voice of the Chicano experience, "Speak Up, Chicano, Speak Up," seeks to abolish social injustice and to bring about a "regeneración" of *la raza*. The word of the individual and social selves, and love, then, are the means to a feeling of plenitude, to an intense feeling that brings a sense of duration within the flow of all things ephemerable.

Taken metaphorically, silence is tantamount to a death-in-life. As an existential proposition, the failure to affirm one's

7

existence is to condemn oneself to oblivion. It is in this metaphorical and existential sense that the goal of self-realization finds its major complement in Villanueva's socially committed poetry. In this context, the oppressor is a majority society that, armed with sound, attempts to make silent victims of *la raza*. The section of poetry entitled *History I Must Wake To* indicates Villanueva's awareness as a voice of the collective *raza*. He speaks for and to his people, inspiring them with hope and urging them to proclaim existence so as to overcome a history of enforced silence and social abnegation. By means of the spoken word, *la raza* can rise from the "shadow of Nothingness," can release itself from "that neverending Nada of servitude." The dialect between the personal and the social indicates that the poet must act in both capacities in order to achieve complete realization of existence

As in his first book, Villanueva's *Shaking Off The Dark* establishes an odyssey from the inner world of the self to the outer world of social conflicts. The first section is subtitled *Much* and consists of ten poems in which the main theme is the breaking of silence and the affirmation of the individual self by means of the creative act. The poem "Much" deals with the genesis of poetic awareness: "The breath is alive / with the equal girth of words. / This fist, a tougher lung, / takes up the oracular burden." The "breath" of the poem aspires for the form of words. To put it in analogical terms, since the poem is an allegory, what the soul is to the body, so the poetic numen is to the word. The shaping of the poem, its gestation period, consists of a process similar to the formation of vital organs. Creativity is pointed to by means of a vigorous metonymy: what breathing is to the lung, so writing is to the fist. This is the "oracular burden." The difficulty inherent in the creative act is underlined by the noun "burden" and the epithet "tougher." The latter also suggests the power of the written word.

The fist, formerly a lung, now becomes a heart as well, palpitating in the creative act: "Fist of my life,/ you are now a heart of light / seeking the good." The tension created between writing and force, which the fist suggests—conceived as a struggle not only to write, the esthetic event, but also as an act of defiance against destruction—finds its complement in the affirmation of an ethical end: "seeking the good."

With this allegory of poetic creation and the resolution of esthetic and ethical ends, that is, the taking of a moral consciousness as well as a poetic one, we note two things. The first, and most obvious, is the process of poetic creation, the engendering of a poem; the second, which we perceive alluded to in the poem's conclusion and confirmed in other poems, is that the poem is born from and unto a literary tradition. Poetry is born of poetry; it is a chain-of-being. In various poems Villanueva acknowledges this fact. He takes pride in revealing his sources and creating his poetry from the ferment of others.

The central images of creativity and revelation for Villanueva, as noted in "Much," are light and water, in their various manifestations. The presence of the former is noted in "Something Beyond Light," where the speaker moves toward a "Horizon / cleared of mist." The landscape of poetry is a *locus amoenus*, a place of tranquility and an eternal present that enables the speaker to discover "names worth saving" and to order "stages of my life." On the edge of poetic illumination, silence is broken, creativity surges on the page, the words come instantaneously:

I am called to by something beyond light:
Everything matters,
feels more generous, alive.
I see
as I've never seen before.
In this long shimmering present,
I write out my heart's memory,
tell stories
under the spell of my own senses.
Line by line
I break silence
with words too sudden to refuse.

This "something beyond light" is a "grace / that keeps giving," and which is illuminated by the creative eye. The poet employs "grace" in three ways, each directly bearing on his goal and profession. The first, aside from its strictly theological aceptance, is that virtue given man for his regeneration—the regenerating power of the word; the second is a privilege—the poetic gift; and the third is fitness or proportion of line or expression—the poem as a formal object, the artifact.

Water imagery is noted in "Of a Parable a Day," where the speaker relates his encounter with a river nymph, the diaphanous and flowing encarnation of poetry. He entreats the nymph to take him with her, but is left on the river's edge, on the shore of creativity, feeling the force of the poetic current. Once created, the poem flows away, so the speaker finds himself "reduced to this: / lonely maker / of a parable a day." The poetic act, then, replenishes the self but the poet must return to these shores in the ritual of self-perpetuation, for "should the whole world / go dark without song /... words / bring back the hymn of meaning /

send ripples through ponds" ("Resolution, I").

In the thirteen poems that comprise the second section subtitled *Odyssey*, Villanueva continues with the theme of creativity. Here Time and Death are not only metaphorical opponents but also the real forces of silence and destruction. As the subtitle suggests, the poet begins to emerge in the world outside the self. In this world the poet encounters scenes and events that parallel his inner struggles.

With "Now that I'm in Spain" the personal labor involved in breaking silence is seen in a political context, the Franco era that spread the fear of speech. Given this concrete reality, reinforced by the ominous rifles of the Guardia Civil, a casual stroll along La Gran Vía belies the fact that the artist is condemned to silence: "They have lined my tongue against a concrete, / diaphanous wall." The poetic voice of art and truth is savaged by the voice of destruction; and the speaker wonders if the commander of García Lorca's execution can himself now speak, if not paralyzed by the horror of his action, or indeed has himself been silenced to hide the truth: "that blast of truth keeps ringing in my ear." Whereas in public the only time the speaker can part his lips is to sip sangría, in the darkness of his hotel room, away from "general eyes," he gives himself to the "secret heights" of poetry. He speaks on the page but hopes "no one knocks at the door."

In "Contaré de un difunto" death is a mirror, "el mejor espejo." The deceased functions as an *exemplum* set forth before the living, saying "This is death, prepare for it." The irony is that the living fail to understand the lesson: "No comprendimos / y nos echamos a reír." Although the survivors laugh in the face of death, what is perceived is death's total negation, stripping away any thought of the consolation of an after-life. The deceased lies dumb, with a still tongue and a hard palate, a sepulchre of a thousand rigid dates. For the poet this is himself—even alive—if he succumbs to silence, if he fails to generate words of flesh, bone and spirit.

"Now, As We Drop: A Poem of Guilt" is dedicated to Anne Sexton. On the advice of her analyst, Sexton began writing poetry as therapy, discharging pent-up emotions through the creative act. Her therapeutic benefit from poetry, then, is consistent with Villanueva's vision of poetry; it is "therapy," it is the untangling of an image which straightens out one's life. Poetry is a sanctuary, "a resting place on one's private journey." It is a constant battle against Death, who grants life grudgingly line-by-line. For Sexton, the therapy wore off. Tired of it all, she chose to cheat Death. If we are to claim consistency of meaning for Villanueva's imagery (light, water, "sacred height"), then Sexton's act of suicide can be taken, paradoxically, as a self-affirmation similar to that which motivates the struggle of the poetic act: "you summoned Death, / and finally you broke into the clear, / rowing into the current waters / toward the tall-drawn / horizon."

In the title poem, "Shaking Off the Dark," the poet reacts against the doldrums of inactivity which have overcome him. Menaced by a hostile world, the "shook heart of a ruined age" can easily be enticed to a passive life and go unresistingly with the flow of time. The poet rebells against this temptation that would commit him to a shadowed existence. He shakes off the dark and the commonplace radiates with song:

I ram a fist into the howl of the wind,
shake off the dark locked
within the hell of these rare depths.
The common street
and shifting sky become a song.

The contemplative attitude and the esthetic event are weapons against time and the dread of dying in obscurity. They are also a moral duty. One must not quit, especially the writer (and here we sense a visceral reaction to Sexton's suicide) who can live by the word and line:

No praise for women like that
nor men
who've lost triumphant eyes,
who've quit the quick of words
with which they might have
raged forever
for a line.

From Silence is a sequence of five love poems which dramatize the movement from the self and the fusion with the other. In these poems it is possible to take the love act as synonymous with the poetic act, as both share the same end of emerging from silence: "You move unto my eyes; / I emerge from silence" ("From Silence"). Love is the creation of a privileged space; it is a poetic moment that allows the lovers to share "the strength of all things flowing" ("Doing Away With Absence"). And as the mist of confusion dissolves before the light of the poetic vision, so a woman's body is revealed to luminous fingers as a landscape: "tus pechos—/ alcanzados / por los soles de mis yemas / son ya colinas descubiertas" ("Así"). The imagery of light and water are also instrumental in the description of the beloved. In the speaker's

arms she is "una cálida lluvia perfumada / transparente."
Consequently, she is a source of poetry and confirms existence, as
that river on whose shores the poet is "bathed in spray" ("Of a
Parable a Day").

The twenty-eight poems that precede the final section of
History I Must Wake To are evenly divided between English and
Spanish. This linguistic symmetry is a clear indication of the
bicultural make-up of Tino Villanueva, and which he calls
"bi-sensibility." The Chicano moves within two cultures, one
which is inherited, the Mexican, and the Anglo-American, which
is assimilated and in which he receives his formal education.
Given this bicultural formation, the Chicano can react in two ways
to the same reality; he has a double sensibility.

Villanueva affirms that for the Chicano this bi-sensibility is at
"the center of our existence." In the *persona* of the Chicano, the
poet moves out of the self and interacts with society. This interac-
tion involves sociopolitical and linguistic realities. Of the twelve
poems that comprise the section of *History I Must Wake To*, two
are in Spanish, five in English and five are bilingual.

With the initial poem of this section, "Haciendo apenas la
recolección," a trek begins in the speaker's memory to his origin
in Texas. The interlingual tension in this corpus of poetry is
immediately noted in the poem's title, where there is a play on
the Spanish word "recolección," in the sense of "cosecha,"
harvest, and the English "to recollect." "Recolección" has two
functions: one literal, cotton picking, and the second, reinforcing
the English, a metaphor for the gathering of memory: "For
weeks now / I have not been able / to liberate me from my name. /
Always I am history I must wake to."

Villanueva's poetry of the Chicano experience is not simply a
"moral gesture" to speak to and for his people. It is a committed
poetry in which we often note the voice of wrath. Yet this commit-
ment does not imply an abandonment of esthetic values. If propa-
ganda literature fails, it is not because it is "propaganda," but
rather because it is quite simply bad literature. Villanueva's
engagé poetry employs rhetoric in the good sense of the word: it
pleases formally, it moves, it affirms, it persuades. Esthetic and
ethical values complement each other. Villanueva conceives engagé
literature as a "combative artistic creation," adding that "to be
an engagé artist is to assume an attitude that the poet lives
ethically and relives esthetically with the aim of condemning
reality and assailing injustice."

In "la recolección" we note a teluric force. In addition to the
imagery of light and water, which occasionally ceases to be meta-

phorical in this section, the presence of the land is felt in the images of dust, sand and wind. Villanueva's poetry operates between two conceptions of dust. There is the dust settled in the memory of his youth which, when "descalzo en angostas calles polvorosas," he carried "shifting in the cuffs of my fading jeans" ("Jugábamos/We Played"). And there is the dust which Time grinds of his bones; the end is Death to which his "dust-bound youth" is destined. In the interim of his *dust-to-dust*, Villanueva attempts to salvage the two entities of his being. Time and Death will eventually pulverize the individual's voice, yet even in life there are oppressive forces whose weapons of sound and dust suffocate a people's voice: "a corrosive dust set loose / by the official attitude of Health Department trucks: / I've tasted that official dust from which / official voices have appeared to thunder."

The recollection of going north to pick cotton assaults the present and causes the speaker's writing arm to become again the picking arm that tensed at the anticipation of painful labor. After the picking the family returned home, which the speaker relives again in his memory. The arm relaxes, his hands will no longer curl in pain: "Weep no more, my common hands; / you shall not again / pick cotton." Paradoxically, his hands are not "common," since they are no longer employed in stoop-labor, yet they now have a *common cause*. With this adjective, the poet asserts his identity as *raza*. Although these hands will never again have to pick cotton, they will labor over Art so as to proclaim the existence of his people: "my strength is flowing." Three poems deal with the various ways by which a majority society can impose silence and vassalage. Psychological pressure can attempt to make the Chicano acquiesce to a feeling of inferiority ("Not Knowing, in Aztlán"). The educational system, instead of stimulating self-expression, only gags the Chicano youth. "Jesús loses his identity in the classroom and becomes "Jesse" who "can't seem to verbalize" ("Chicano Dropout"). Besides the educational, there is also state-sanctioned violence. In "Non-Ode to the Texas Rangers," the frame of reference is the use of "rinches" as strike breakers. The attempt to earn better wages and to share in the American Dream is gunned down at "pointblank."

Another theme in this section is the tribute paid to the forefathers of *la raza* who did not have a *movimiento* to support them. "Now, Suns Later" is an elegy to the poet's grandmother, conceived as an archetype as well: "that yielding belly put nine screaming mouths / at a simple table. / . . . / kneading *tortillas* / to keep a race going." The grandmother brings light in the sense of giving birth, "da luz," but she also stands in the light. Under the

13

"arrogant sun" she brings her fertility to the fields where crops spring from the tilled earth. Yet she too is "arrogant," as she defies the sun's heat "finding her place." The function and frequency of light imagery confirms that the grandmother shares in the sun's force; she is a source of energy, a *mater genetrix*.

The predominantly figurative function of the water imagery in the previous sections, like the light imagery, is in the poetry of this section both metaphorical and real. The grandmother advancing in age is the "solitary washer" who at once cleans the family's clothes of the corroding earth, "regenerating" the family and forestalling their bodies' inevitable corrosion; she is the washer who at once rinses the windows and makes the outdoors sparkle. Finally, by means of the word, the grandmother cleanses the soul and stores in the children's mind that history neglected by the educational system.

The book's final poem, "Speak Up, Chicano, Speak Up," was first published as a broadside. As a poetic broadcast, it took the voice of protest to the streets. Here the poem's intention, the original medium and the addressee determine its language and structure. This poem is characterized by its oratory discourse, and as such it reminds us of the oral tradition of Chicano literature. Taken as oratory, the poem is deliberative because its intention is to exhort, to rouse a people to action: "You must act to be free." The poet as orator affirms that only by *voicing* their right to a full existence can his people begin to live: "The problem is we live by other people's words: / We think we are what *they* think we are."

Shaking Off The Dark, as a complement to its linguistic symmetry, displays a remarkable trajectory. With the book's initial poem, we note the first essay of a voice determined to confirm the existence of the individual by means of self-expression. At the conclusion we perceive an oratory voice vehemently affirming a society's right to exist. The final poem urges the Chicano to *speak up* for himself. Tino Villanueva, at this pole of his poetic and ethical actions, is now willing to give up his voice.

Tino Villanueva's new collection of poetry arrives a little more than a decade after *Hay Otra Voz Poems*, his first book. *Shaking Off The Dark* is a book for which we have waited too long.

Julián Olivares
Editor, *Revista Chicano-Riqueña*
Houston, 21.I.84

MUCH

Much

The breath is alive
with the equal girth of words.
This fist, a tougher lung,
takes up the oracular burden.
For whom this rage,
this fever of the evening?
And how much does it matter
that I choose
the shadows of words,
unloose the archetypes of fire
and water?
Fist of my life,
you are now a heart of light
seeking the good.

But much is yet to be recovered,
much to be begun.
Here the trek begins in earnest
sense by sense.

Something Beyond Light

Horizon
cleared of mist,
claiming part beauty, part dreams.
I move toward it
in search of names worth saving,
ordering stages of my life
within the grace
that keeps giving.
Unbounded, the landscape
and the simple stones
shudder in dawn's cast.

I accept this endless peace.

I am called to by something beyond light:
Everything matters,
feels more generous, alive.
I see
as I've never seen before.
In this long shimmering present,
I write out my heart's memory,
tell stories
under the spell of my own senses.
Line by line
I break silence
with words too sudden to refuse.

Destrucreación

Fiebre y más fiebre como si me hubieran besado entre sábanas y sueños: invasión que me empaña las perspectivas ya encontradas. Se me desintegra la memoria, pero sé que por lo menos me aproximo a un punto de partida. De aquí me llegaré a donde voy. Todo es fructífera locura, destrucreación, autosuficiencia, culto al que asisto con frecuencia. Vicio que me ampara.

Existencias

Pensar decir tachar/añadir certezas.
Borrar después con precisión para empezar
por el comienzo:

   queda un latido en cada reinicio,
   un ardor
   casi palpable.

Ante el Cuadro de Picasso *Les Plastrons*, 1901

(en el Museo de Bellas Artes, Boston)

La escena es turbia y apagada;
el momento, transparente.
No hay
ni habrá secretos en penumbra
porque está para moverse en clímax,
de arriba a abajo,
el silencio en ella perfilado.

Interesan los más cercanos
que ante el proscenio
extienden sus miradas.
Llaman la atención sus cándidos plastrones
reteblancos, almidonados que un fuego
verdadero ocultan.

Y el sabor rodando va
gota a gota
en infinitos paladares,
y en las tinieblas se contuerce
quietamente la tibieza de sus muslos prohibidos.
Así tendrá que ser

ante ella

que con su clara mano franca
intenta desnudarse.

Recital

A Jorge Guillén

Todo
lo que significa invencible manantial,
candor,
instante de fulgor vivo,
lo trajiste
en aquel atardecer de atardeceres
al fiel recinto de la ofrendada
y extática palabra.
Cantaste
y nos llamaste a los senderos de tus años
de luz exaltadora.
Cuán rauda manera de aligerar el viaje:
cada uno a su fe dejándose llevar,
latido
por latido,
al duradero centro
de todo lo que existe.
¿Quién más que tú,
ha podido enteramente revelar,
palabra
sobre
perpetua palabra,
el universo inalcanzable
y sorprendentemente nuestro?
Esto es vivir ante la luz plural del sol
que cae y nunca cae en esta tarde;
esto es vivir
en el alto sitio de la flúida creación,
porque más que claridad sonora
eres, has sido,
serás
presencia.

La obra visible*

Of a Parable a Day

As if from a river
far away and
shimmering in a continent
warm and undiscovered,
you came drifting
all the while toward me, with the slim moon
placidly rippling in your wake.

Those too eager to explain
might have imagined you at best
an apparition,
the kind a person knows
once only
in a lifetime.

Dreamers too readily convinced
might have seen clear through you,
and known your true and sacred lineage;
foretold, even, the steady route you finally took.

Still others too easily entertained
might have mistaken you for
just another nymph at dusk,
or a mermaid teasing the shore.

But I, searcher always of
secrets of the wild,
wanted to understand you up close,
wished to follow alongside your
smooth thigh
and try everything the water knows
to buoy you up for however long you drifted.

"Take me with you," I called out, already
bathed in spray.
But your parting was so swift: Your splendid

figure cut against the widening sky.
"I mean no harm," I yelled,
seeming ever to reach
for the river's charm.

And rounding the bend
past the gently waving evergreens
you were now cast in new light,
and calling back: "Let me journey to no end.
I'm not who you think I am.
And besides, my good man, if I must live
my life over again,
so I must follow toward the sun,
and come back as more."

So I am here, reduced to this:
lonely maker
of a parable a day,
lover of twilights and dawns;
questioning myself aloud,
minding the right words,
and asking what being you possess.
I am summoned often
to these everlasting shores.
Here I shall let no one distract me
from your tempting flow,
no one dissuade me from the vision that I hold.

Resolution, I

I shall chase away
the tenous ghosts
from a year ago,
sprout questions I myself
cannot answer.
And toward evening,
should the whole world
go dark without song
above the tree line
of my city,
with silence drifting
on water instead of light,
then too will words
bring back the hymn of meaning,
send ripples through ponds.

Resolution, II

Nowhere shall it be written
I cannot write into these lines
pity, lamentation and wild joy,
shift the layers of time
before the morning light,
or against a low sun
in an ochre afternoon.

Already many things have changed.

ODYSSEY

Ensueño

Disparar contra un reloj de torre:
se detendría el instante;
quedaría cristalizado,
desconcretado,
el tiempo irrepetible—

y sobre todo

autónomo.

Retorno

En rotación: inmóvil mediodía—

    solitaria y perseguida manecilla

(y sobre todo)
acosada por la instantánea medianoche
que rotundamente llega
y reanuda
su búsqueda encontrada.

And The Forecast For Today . . .

Bruma matinal
    entre nubes y calles enmarañadas
    entre aceras y parques sostenidos
    por inevitables raíces.

Voy por esta permanencia
de arremolinados instantes de viento y vendaval,
de indecisa luz por donde no se deja ver
ni el semáforo más cercano.

Ni a mí me veo.

Now That I'm In Spain

(Reflections of Madrid, Summer 1969)

They have lined my tongue against a concrete,
diaphanous wall:

    the many rifles at the crossroads
    where the careful traffic goes,
    and general eyes are blazing
    from behind
    Don Quixote at the Plaza de España.

In a crossfire of glances
I stroll La Gran Vía wondering if he
who burst ¡*FUEGO*! at Federico's blood
has his voice still—
that blast of truth keeps ringing in my ear.

On Sundays I examine El Rastro.
Its threatening 1936 rust is ever-rugged.
Better to sit at sidewalk cafes to conjecture
the origins of tourists.
The only time I part my lips is to sip sangría;
then once in my secret heights I embrace the dark,
and hope no one knocks at the door.

Odyssey
(On the NY Thruway)

On your own you know to a degree,
the open measured road:

your everyday limited at your
own speed;
longitude and latitude converging,
and in a breath you realize
the horizon keeps outlasting your vision,
as fleet trees blaze by growing into oblivion.

And you will pass this way
again
not knowing the unrivaled time of day,
nor when to panic.

El primero de enero

En rigor
a tiempo llega
cargado de abriles disfrazados

Inesperadamente
cae
en cierto día cierto
como un resucitado calendario.

Sol

Escalofríos de verano:

de caminante voy
bajo
pleno sol
que nace
crece
decae y renace.

Sin adelantarse
retrocede incansablemente
hacia adelante
con la misma furia de antes.

Contaré de un difunto

Aquí el recién finado, el mejor espejo.

Tras sus párpados palpables:
    mil rígidas fechas;
    inmóviles memorias de algún viaje postergado.

Tras sus arrugas afeitadas:
    aterida sangre transparente;
    duro paladar y subjuntiva lengua.

Apenas ayer habías dicho: *He tomado conciencia*
    de que soy contemporáneo de todos
    los hombres.

No comprendimos
y nos echamos a reír.

To Budding Roses

In this green month
when you are uncaressable
still
budding at every turning second
to burst into our fragile eyes
to spring into our first cupped touch—

you are so ignorant of death.

Now, As We Drop: A Poem Of Guilt

for Anne Sexton, 1928-1974

It was for therapy you sang
from the wounded house.
It had come to that:
releasing passion from the fist;
working both ends of the clock
to death.
And those tangled images
kept coming in volumes
slim and loud.
How each poem became a resting place
on one's private journey;
how each time your breath kissed us awake.
And for awhile you
straightened out the image,

sharing it like homemade bread;
like balloons ten for a quarter.
Then the tension broke;
the cords snapped,
so you summoned what made you feel
more alive: you summoned Death,
and finally you broke into the clear,
rowing into the current waters
toward the tall-drawn
horizon framed weak for a steeple;
rowing, rowing always against the dark,
for nothing must have been lit
in the sacred height.
And there you were, engulfed in the Fall,

confessedly wrecked and undone by the fumes
of the hurried act: you against Death
Death against you
you against you

hearing Death grinding his engine,
feeling Death climbing up
your limp breath;
Death, oh tasteless Death, coming
with his pale-blue eyes.
And choosing to live no more for a line
you braved it all the way,
preferring heresy to pain,
living up to your final word, that sullen act:
and *that* is no sin before any God.

But we are the Death-dealers: we who once
read your life and bought your image.
Now, as we drop
toward our sound dreams,
we toss with guilt,
and turn tangled in our sheets
as your profile cuts our sleep.

Shaking Off The Dark

I am less constant
in this cold wind that does not rise,
that does not rest.
Thoughts fall over with sleep
I cannot command.
Shook heart of the ruined age
is what I've become.

Distraught,
mad-eyed from told formulas
bound to rule my easy ways,
I look, I see,
but fail once more to know.
Such rites of life
can waste the wit;
can be like strictures
rushing to the head.
Mine is a palpable body
that cannot stand itself.

Yet, a rebellion overtakes the mind,
the kind that breaks the shadow's hold:
I ram a fist into the howl of the wind,
shake off the dark locked
within the hell of these rare depths.
The common street
and shifting sky become a song.

I've come to rest on a conviction:
No praise for women like that
nor men
who've lost triumphant eyes,
who've quit the quick of words
with which they might have
raged forever
    for a line.

Again

So I depend again upon myself.
I've taught this part of me
to go unruined
through all enormous lessons
on defeat.
I've taught this part of me
to thrive among despair,
to be imperative
among chaotic numbers.
Though I may fall away from time to time
like draggled weeds in winter,
breathing thick stern air
in some back shadows of the walk,
I spring again from me,
from the dead quiet of my roots—
listen to me move.

By dawn
I am presence fixed
in the eyes of men.

Persistent Dream

In a calm persistent dream
I am crossing the shore,
as the on-going light of stars
settles over the waters
of my voyage.
What this river does
cannot be forgotten,
for something of myself says
I am moving among bright mist,
tells me I could go on forever
through the woods I am entering
as I would my life.

FROM SILENCE

From Silence

You move unto my eyes;
I emerge from silence.
Adrift on our spirit
as we do the fond dance

—as natural as breathing in
and breathing out—

and empty ourselves of praise,
we do not dissolve in the truth
of our calm,
in the soothing touch
of nightfall upon the earth.

Doing Away With Absence

Drawn each to each
in some arrangement of ourselves
we are lifted
away from twilight,

and elsewhere

we are going hand in hand by a river,
naming the strength of all things flowing.
As we advance, unhurried,
telling each other our best truths,
a moon sweeps out
         serenely for miles around.

To you, and through us,
love is kind.

Así

Así
   de lejos
      son niebla
         tus pechos—

alcanzados
      por los soles de mis yemas
son ya colinas descubiertas.

Entre mis brazos

Eres
   entre mis brazos
   una cálida lluvia perfumada
           transparente
           desvestida.

Así llegar

Algún día llegará la aurora
más acá de muchas noches ilusorias.
Así llegar

    a ti quisiera

como el saludable sol a la mañana:
rodearte de tibia luz primero,
para en ti después poner un sólo ardor.

HISTORY I MUST WAKE TO

Haciendo apenas la recolección

For weeks now
I have not been able
to liberate me from my name.
Always I am history I must wake to.
In idiot defeat I trace my routes
across a half-forgotten map of Texas.
I smooth out the folds stubborn
as the memory.

Let me see: I would start from San Marcos,
moving northward,
bored beyond recognition
in the stale air of a '52 Chevy:
to my left, the youngest of uncles
steadies the car;
to my right, grandfather finds humor
in the same joke.
I am hauled among family
extended across the back seat,
as the towns bury themselves forever
in my eyes: Austin, Lampasas, Brownwood,
past Abilene, Sweetwater,
along
the Panhandle's alien tallness.
There it is: Lubbock sounding harsh as ever.
I press its dark letters,
and dust on my fingertips is so alive
it startles them
as once did sand.
Then west, 10,000 acres and a finger's breadth,
is Levelland
where a thin house once stood,
keeping watch over me and my baseball glove
when the wrath of winds cleared the earth
of stooping folk.
There's Ropesville, where in fifth grade
I didn't make a friend.

My arm is taut by now and terrified.
It slackens,
begins falling back into place,
while the years are gathering slowly
along still roads and hill country,
downward
to where it all began—500 McKie Street.
I am home, and although the stars
are at rest tonight,
my strength is flowing.

Weep no more, my common hands;
you shall not again
pick cotton.

March 1979-January 1980

I Too Have Walked My Barrio Streets

Andando por San Antonio arriba
vi la quietud de la pobreza:
rechinaban los goznes quebrados,
las puertas cansadas querían
ir a sollozar o a dormir.

....

Se preparaba para el fuego
la madera de la pobreza.

"*Arrabales (Canción Triste)*"
Pablo Neruda

I too have walked my barrio streets,
seen life not worth the lingering grief.

(As a child and migrant,
I've picked clean straight rows of cotton
when the Summers were afire.
And driven by hunger, I've come face to face
with the uprooted fury of the West Texas wind.
I've slept on floors of Winter's many corners,
on linoleum-covered dirtfloors
of the hard-sprawled Panhandle.
I've taken refuge under cowsheds
when all of driving Winter rained down a sea
of stiff mud.)

I too have walked my barrio streets,
smelled patio flowers burning in the stabbing sun,
and those in grandma's flower-pots are weary flowers
that do not wilt, instead, they're crushed
by bitter dust from streets forgotten,
a corrosive dust set loose
by the official attitude of Health Department trucks:
I've tasted that official dust from which
official voices have appeared to thunder:

Yore outhouse's gotta go. It's unsanitary, and b'sides,
The City of San Marcos is askin' all of y'all with
outhouses ta git inside plumbin'. After all, y'all've
had a drainage system come through heah for the last
three years. Ya got one month ta do it in. OK, amigo?

(I've printed my name at different schools
for indifferent teachers
who've snickered at my native surname,
who've turned me in "for speaking Spanish on
      the premises"
long before Jamestown,
and so I've brightly scrawled transcending obscenities
in adolescent rage.)

I too have walked my barrio streets,
gone among old scars and young wounds
who, gathering at the edge of town, on nearby corners,
mend their broken history with their timely tales.

(I've been quizzed on Texas history—
history contrived in dark corridors
by darker still textbook committees.
I've read those tinged white pages where the ink
went casting obscurantism across the page:
the shadows had long dried into a fierce solid state.
And Bigfoot Wallace had always been my teacher's hero,
and what's worse, I believed it,
oh, how we all believed it.)

I too have walked my barrio streets,
seen over-worked and hollow-eyed men
in the unemployment line, their wrinkled bodies worked-over
like the sharecropped furrows they once grew
under day-long mules steady as the plowing sun.

(With many others,
I've thrust a picket sign into the chanting Boston air:

Work's too hard,
pay's too low,
Farah pants have got to go!
I've struck down
what Farah slacks
were hanging on the racks, and down the street,
what sold-out lettuce came to the sell-out counters
of the East:
¡Obreros unidos,
jamás serán vencidos!)

I too have walked my barrio streets,
heard those congenial strangers
who put up their finest drawl in yearly, murdered Spanish!

    Voutin poar mey. Yeu soay eil meijoar keindideitou
    para seyerveerleis.

But somewhere in the bred fever of the barrio,
Carmelita López, in a sad dress, clutches the warmth
of her raggedy doll;
Carmelita cries out for milk, and so drowns out
the paid political pronouncement.
Carmelita, with the languid frame,
shrivels in November's fever, and her laid-off *papi*
can only wish to fix the roof that sprung a leak
a year or two ago.

Pablo, I too have walked my barrio streets.
And this I say: that in our barrio,
where a whole country is a parody of itself,
there's still plenty of wood to burn,
and that the winds of the people
are keeping all flames aglow,
until the mighty hand that holds dominion over
    Man is bent back at the finger joints;
until the swivel chairs of official leather

are rooted out from thickly-soiled, pile carpets;
until all pain is driven out at last from the naked barrio.

Walking around.
So many times we've walked along
interminable streets, Pablo.
Yet one loud question keeps pounding in my ear:

A poet's devotion, can't it reach beyond mere walking,
beyond found words
when the people are stirring into the glowing wind?

Nuestros Abuelos

*Who are the plaintiffs? It is the conquered who are humbled before the conqueror asking for his protection, while enjoying what little their misfortune has left them . . . They do not understand the prevalent language of their native soil. They are strangers in their own land.**

Nuestros abuelos
in their private suffering
toiled
between the four winds of heaven
& the fifth sun.

Sus espaldas carried ties
for iron-horse companies;
sus coyunturas genuflected
for other similar go-West-young-man
enterprises.

Sus manos se hincharon de años
y de callos y por eso
sus cuerpos,
cansadas cicatrices,
han llegado
hasta la humilde tumba.

---

*The Honorable Don Pablo de la Guerra, April 26, 1856, in opposition to the "law to settle land titles in California," approved by the legislature in 1856; from *El Grito*, Vol. V, No. 1 (Fall 1971).

Variation
on a
Theme by William Carlos Williams

I have eaten
the *tamales*
that were on
the stove heating

and which
you were probably
having
for dinner

Perdóname
they were *riquísimos*
so juicy
and so steaming hot.

Jugábamos/We Played

en el barrio
—en las tardes de fuego
when the dusk prowls
en la calle desierta
pues los jefes y jefas
trabajan
—often late hours
after school
we play canicas . . .

Alurista

The memories of childhood have no
order, and no end.

Dylan Thomas

jugábamos/saltábamos/
jugábamos a todo.
era rito y recreación en el patio de mi barrio
in the just-awakening week: kneeling there
in sunnybronzed delight
when my kingdom was a pocketful of
golden marbles.
how in wide-eyed wonder i sought winning
two agates for my eyes/& so,
not knowing what it meant, i played for keeps.

*****

jugábamos/y nos jugábamos la vida—
    my posse always got its man/
    i was the Chicano Lone Ranger/i was Tarzan
    of backyard pecan trees/time-tall trees blooming
    with the color of adventure/trees that ripened
    with my age through rain-ruined days.

running/gamboling i played oblivious to
fine earth shifting in the cuffs of my fading jeans/

61

crawling/leaping always reaching/
alcanzando/alcanzando hasta las delicias del vacío
indomable/
corriendo por los rincones de mi patio
donde mi abuela tenía sembrado tulipanes y claveles/
correteando por entre sol y resolanas
en aquellas tardes de aquel fuego.

jugábamos/brincábamos/
jugábamos a todo.
era mito y sensación when the tree-house wind blew
in simultaneous weathers: era un viento verde
sabor a higo, a hierbabuena, a veces a durazno—

      esencias de nuestro jardín.

and in my Cracker-Jack-joy of late saturday afternoons
my red wagon was full of dog/& my tricycle traveled
one last time every turnpike of my yard.

now the fun running to soothe the dry sun on my tongue/
now the tireless striding toward stilled water of
buoyant ice cubes in a glass transparent dripping
in the grip of my mother's hand.

            ******

jugábamos/corríamos
jugábamos a todo.
era grito y emoción en mi predilecto pasatiempo:

      thirteen years out of the womb i was
      pubescent Walter Mitty fleet as Mickey Mantle
      at the Stadium:

      tok! . . . there's a long drive to center . . . Villanueva
      is back/back/the ball is up against the wall . . .

as i banged my back against our dilapidated
picket fence
(grandpa repaired it twelve times over)
yes, i dreamed of spikes and baseball diamonds/
meantime
i played descalzo en angostas calles polvorosas
(a dust decreed by the City Council, i know now)
mis camaradas in bubble-gum smiles chose up sides/
so batter up 'cause i'm a portsider like
Whitey Ford/i've the eagle eye of Ted Williams.
i tugged the bill of my sea-blue cap for luck/
had NY on it:

time out! let the dust settle,
traffic should slow down on gravel streets—
especially Coca-Cola trucks.

but the game goes on/dust mixing with perspiration.
inning after inning this game becomes a night game too/
this 100-watt bulb lights the narrow playing field.

******

such were the times of year-rounded yearnings
when at the end of light's flight i listened in
reflective boyhood silence.
then the day-done sun glistened, burned deeply,
disappearing into my eyes blinking: innocently
i blinked toward the towering twilight.

jugábamos/saltábamos/
jugábamos a todo.

Paris, September 2, 1972

Not Knowing, in Aztlán

the way they look at you
the schoolteachers
the way they look at you
the City Hall clerks
the way they look at you
the cops
the airport marshals
the way they look at you

you don't know if it's something you did

or something you are.

Chicano Dropout

Jesús.

In another world lo bautizaron, *Jesse*—
     era el más chuco de todos.

But no one, nadie
     (ni el más sabelotodo supo de su historia):

He doesn't bother participating in my history class.
He can't seem to verbalize in our speech class, you know.
Tino, just what's wrong with these Latin Americans?

So Jesse,
     cuando era junior, was pushed out into
     dirty-brown streets of his zip-coded barrio.

He left quietly,
     but on his desk he left carved his name: **CHUY**

Non-Ode To The Texas Rangers

*. . . the Rangers among Mexican Americans
have a good reputation.**

A. Y. Allee, Captain, Texas Rangers

*Pasan, si quieren pasar,
y ocultan en la cabeza
una vaga astronomía
de pistolas inconcretas.*

"Romance de la Guardia Civil española"
Federico García Lorca

Day breaks raw
under siege. Time strikes dumb the dawn
down the broad-shouldered Interstate—

make way
for the lone-tin-stars spangling the shrouded myth/
fleet machines
driven by double-brute barreling
down/
through/
up/
into post-1848 *barrios*—ovens of tragedian Valley.

Again to murder Spanish and the tongue/
murder incorporated
into your glance/your long-range aim is clear/
no questions asked/
mobile chambers of justice at pointblank
gunning
down
also the mind
in front of El Buen Redentor Baptist Church/
we have witnesses/
choir members came chorally screaming:

¡Socorrio! Tres rinches, one riot!

We've been told this news before
on this same unpaved crossroads where
bicultural dreams are shattered:

> had just returned from *las piscas*
> this man of the soil—Pancho Anónimo was/is
> his name/gypsy-bronzed/
>
> caught in the flash of leaded wind/
> his hands were in his pocket but the
> blast blew loose his stride &
> stunned him still in a pool of splash/
> there's gravel or is it shrapnel in his stare.
>
> Another borderline case but his wounds
> are deeper than blood three pints full
> soaking & seeding our soil.

******

Without warning
then & there
you leave behind
one Spring day hemorrhaging
under metallic-blue sky/high wide sky
gauzed with Andalusian clouds—only your damn bluebonnets
are left intact.

******

I still maintain:

my scars shall haunt your children/
Chicano blood shall ransom
pint
by
pint
the blood shed here/

or my skin's not brown.

*Hearings, U.S. Commission on Civil Rights, San Antonio,
Texas, December 14, 1968, from *San Antonio Sunday Express
and News* (December 15, 1968)

Fábula de aquella lluvia que arreció

Aquella lluvia que arreció su inesperada furia,
abrileña y a su vez castigadora,
se negó a darnos tiempo
de ampliamente refugiarnos.
Fue sin duda sumisión, violencia,
casi servidumbre que
pareció durar más allá de muchos días.
Mas cuando aplacó su antiquísimo dominio
todo iba recobrando su luz de antes: saliendo
fuimos por los umbrales todos encendidos;
nada pudo resistir tanta regeneración.
Había, como quien dice, *movimiento*.
Y en cierto modo
fue como ver el origen de las cosas.

Considerando en frío, imparcialmente, César*

Considerando en frío, imparcialmente, César,
que moriste en París sin aguacero,
un día Viernes Santo de primavera,
un día del cual no puedo ya olvidar . . .

Considerando
que gemebundo lamentabas la angustia
de tu espíritu que por 112 días
encarcelaron en Trujillo,
y otra vez quebrantaron
en un sanguinolento julio,
y que por ende, fe en el hombre
habías tú perdido . . .

Comprendiendo sin esfuerzo
que el hombre de mi Raza todavía suda,
pero ahora grita ¡BASTA!
. . . *from sea to shining sea* . . .

Considerando también
que la familia de Davy Crockett se apoderó de Texas,
y Smokey the Bear de Nuevo México;
que nos pegan todos
sin que nosotros les hagamos nada . . .

Examinando, en fin,
nuestro ánimo y ahinco,
aun después de un largo siglo atroz . . .

Comprendiendo
que Corky, José Angel, Dolores Huerta,
Tijerina, Enriqueta Vasquez, y claro,
tu tocayo de Delano,
mas tres aulas llenas de académicos
que ahora nos rescatan para nunca jamás
ser nosotros *criminals of a scholarly society* . . .

Considerando nuestros documentos
y Planes específicos que muestran
que somos una hábil masa inquebrantable . . .

   te hago saber, César, que vamos ganando terreno;
son testigos el quinto sol, los días hábiles,
la piel de bronce, el Carnalismo, los surcos,
el grito audaz y el águila negra.
Y si pudieras ver al Hombre ahora, César,
te quedarías (estoy seguro)
emocionado . . . Emocionado . . .

---

   *Con los siguientes textos a la mano: "Considerando en frío,
imparcialmente" y "Piedra negra sobre una piedra blanca" de
César Vallejo

Now, Suns Later

For my grandmother, Clara Solana Ríos,
Eagle Pass, Texas (1885)—San Marcos,
Texas (1965).

The century heaved a turn
and seven years later she took him
for the life of her.

She made sure granddad arose for the love of her:
that yielding belly put nine screaming mouths
at a simple table.
She left no one unweaned, unwanted;
was up before the sun struck dawn,
kneading *tortillas*
to keep a race going.

And when dawn's colors flooded the lasting fields,
she walked into light
finding her place in the arrogant sun:
she too went tilling the yielding earth.
And to the blazing wind sparks flew
from sun-struck stones
scraped by her quick-thinning hoe.
Her lean, strong digging round the first juices
of cotton: life seeds smothered
in mean temperatures of a hundred.
And after the timely rain she picked it by the baleful,
and when it came back to her,
her threads like rainbows gave shape to warmth.
From ready remnants, she patterned light glowing quilts;
from remnants of remnants, she braided a rug.
And pillows, high and ruffled, came from feathers
of Sunday chickens.

******

The 30s brought her into the city,
but not to rest yet.
How could she, with a family following the sun
round a farm still?
Arm-weary, that solitary washer stooped
because she had to
over her only washboard.
Her slim life bending like a corn stalk,
fragile, in the middle of a Spring wind;
her wringing fingers making clean a family
of wet-wash, freeing it again from earth.
And having hardly rested, before supper,
she rinsed clear the outdoors on window panes.
Then, because everyday was a God,
we assembled at her feet in Bible-black nights,
and heard in Spanish,
the Presbyterian Prophets speak with clarity:
we lingered in her words, and we believed her faith.

When asked about torn history,
she'd squint past you through wrinkles
into that imaginary distance of infinite cottonfields,
recalling:

>   her favorite dawns,
>   the drought of '25,
>   the Christmas of '48 when her three quick sons
>   marched out of the distant seas.

I see her garden, freshturned in an hour's time:
how under the falling light
she goes trimming the twilight of leaves;
caressing buds almost afire;
making a Spring bloom year-round from flowerpots:
her cupped hands kindling a wilting flower back to light.

******

I saw her last in '64
when the Army took me to its cold bivouacs.
Her eyes were sharp with pain.
And she sighed more than usual: ¡Ay, qué afán!, she ached.
"Oh, what a chore!"

A year later, the letter, airmailed from Texas
in mid-March sprouting warm,
spoke of how still our garden had become,
how the quick of the sun came up no more
one sudden-gray and absent morning.

Now, suns later,
on this dawn near freezing with a promise of sure snow:
I am sustained
thinking back how much she strained in radiant need;
and wonder why it had to be that way;
why no Movement pushed to slow down
the strides of the sun for her, that woman,
moving always in rhythms of labor in Texas sprawling days.
Still her memory warms the day for me.
And I endure,
for patience must have been her only strength,
her only movement, truly private.
Lonely.

Boston, Winter, 1974-1975.

Speak Up, Chicano, Speak Up

In broad, back-aching fields;
in sun-blasted vineyards and rough farms;
in shops full of hammers and tools;
in buildings and schools where you sweep
the tedious floors,
scrub, one by one,
the toilets' dark yellow rings;
in the works and days of your existence
where you're paid to break
out in a sweat and break down:
Speak up and tell them!
You're not getting a square deal, you say?
The just-hired *americano* is earning
already more than you, is that it?
Tell them!
Tell them you've been there much longer;
have come to work each day on time,
each week, each year;
have turned in a job done well enough
to clench a decent raise.
But you must tell them! You must.

******

At full stores arranged to fit around
our lives;
at restaurants carefully built
for fine, polished forks;
at factories stacked high
with your singular craft,
done at exhausting swift speeds:
Tell them! No voicer is louder than your own.
You've stayed on
through thick and thin more than enough:
Remind them!
You've offered adroit hands, so complete

and ready to serve—
that alone deserves its reward in better benefits,
don't you think?
> Diles que después de tanto tiempo
> exiges un aumento de salario.
> O como dicen los pachucos: "¡No te dejes, ése.
> Anda y cántales por más feria. Que te paguen
> de aquélla por tu jale, carnal!"
Unbow your head and tell them.
What's wrong, can't you get angry enough?
Still think minding your manners is the best choice?
Care enough to act!
No need to be rude,
just don't be so damn agreeable and polite
all the time: Dare to ask, suggest, challenge.
wear them down if need be—
so it goes with all that's worth defending.
But caution: Don't let your weary anger
blur the mind.
Stand alert and unconquerable instead;
know always from the start
what you're talking about.
Get your facts straight.
Then tell them!

******

And it matters little that you call yourself
mexicano, Mexican American, mexicanoamericano,
hispano, Hispanic American, Spanish American,
Latin American, or Chicano;
or that you are lighter skinned,
speak English with utterly divine diction,
and have won a Congressional Medal of Honor . . .
To them there is no difference.
Your brown last name gives you away.
Aren't we harassed just the same by those
deliberate walls—stout walls reared up

by the army of the One Race?
Speak up, Chicano, and cleanse the dark rage
from the Soul!
Let your authentic voice bring down, one by one,
each wall.
Draw the line now; back down no more.
Be unafraid and tell them!

******

And you, young man, young woman:
Bright youth of the school yards;
freshmen seeing it through; sophomores
and graduates holding your own,
if in class you think you know the answer,
or should have an additional thought
to be considered,
speak up and tell them!
Take account of your own history;
recognize your own worth, then raise your hand
and tell it the best you can.
Make yourself visible.
Make your presence known, my friend,
it matters that you do. *You* matter.

******

So arise, Chicano,
arise from the shadow of Nothingness;
arise from that neverending *Nada* of servitude.
The problem is we live by other people's words:
We think we are what *they* think we are.

Hollywood and Sociologists have tried so hard
to do us in.
So arise and step out
from that long night of denial.
Chicano, don't let the ignorance of Man

command your conscience.
Arise and tell your neighbor the news;
let the few become many.
Remember this: You are *free* to act,
but you must *act* to be free.

******

So what's it going to be: Do we stand,
or remain forever dead and dying?
The matter is not even open to discussion!
Collect the needed facts, double check them—
you're responsible for that, no one else,
Then make yourself a plan.
Above all think it through: A mind without an idea
is like a blind eye that can't see.

******

And so, good friend, whether you pray it once,
twice, or many more,
take with you, forever, this sole meditation
from which must come our strength:

> I am *free* to act, but I must *act* to be free.
> I am *free* to act, but I must *act* to be free.
> I am *free* to act, but I must *act* to be free.

The Author

Tino Villanueva was born in San Marcos, Texas, on December 11, 1941. His parents, after World War II and the Works Progress Administration, were obliged to return to their previous occupation as field workers, which explains Tino's nomadic schoolchild existence. He graduated uneducated from high school having learned virtually nothing except racial prejudice and "Texas History." He then worked in a furniture factory for three years, during which time he began to make up for the gaps in his education. Without realizing the eventual outcome of his autodidacticism, he dedicated himself to self-improvement by studying the "Increase Your Word Power" section of *Reader's Digest*.

Tino was drafted into the Army in 1963 and spent two years in the Panama Canal Zone, where he was brought into closer contact with Hispanic culture and where he first heard of Rubén Darío and José Martí. When he returned to his hometown, he studied Spanish and English at Southwest Texas State University under the V. A. Bill. His English professors recommended he study e. e. cummings, the beatniks, T. S. Eliot and, especially for him, Dylan Thomas. It was under the latter's influence that he wrote one of his first poems, "My Certain Burn Toward Pale Ashes." He began to publish his poetry in the *San Antonio Express/ Evening News*.

After receiving his B. A. in 1969 and after a summer session at the Universidad de Salamanca, Tino went to graduate school at Suny-Buffalo. He read more American and Hispanic poets, but it was *El Espejo/The Mirror* (1969), the first anthology of Chicano literature, that aroused the other half of his sensibility. It was also the distance from the Southwest that permitted him to take stock of and to penetrate and to take into account the lies, prejudice, images and injustices perpetrated upon him and his people. This was the time that he embraced the Chicano Movement.

In 1972 Tino published *Hay Otra Voz Poems*. His literary career and fame began. He continued to publish poetry and literary articles in various journals, and to give readings here and abroad. He received his Ph.D. in Spanish in 1981 from Boston University. He is presently an Assistant Professor of Spanish at Wellesley College.

Tino Villanueva lives in Boston, in a small apartment within walking distance of Fenway Park, but, faithful to his boyhood memories, his favorite team is the New York Yankees. His apartment is full of books—on the floor, chairs and table. Not only has he edited his own anthology of Chicano literature, *Chicanos: antología histórica y literaria* (1980), but he himself is a repository of Chicano history, lore and culture. He knows all the names of the Chicanos who have won the Congressional Medal of Honor. He also makes excellent margaritas.